HOLIDAY
CRAFTS

50 Projects for Year-Round Family Fun

Linda Reece

Skyhorse Publishing

Skyhorse Publishing books may be purchased in bulk at special discounts for sales promotion, corporate gifts, fund-raising, or educational purposes. Special editions can also be created to specifications. For details, contact the Special Sales Department, Skyhorse Publishing, 307 West 36th Street, 11th Floor, New York, NY 10018 or info@skyhorsepublishing.com.

Skyhorse® and Skyhorse Publishing® are registered trademarks of Skyhorse Publishing, Inc.®, a Delaware corporation.

Visit our website at www.skyhorsepublishing.com.

10 9 8 7 6 5 4 3 2

Library of Congress Cataloging-in-Publication Data is available on file.
Cover design by Erin Seaward-Hiatt

Print ISBN: 978-1-63450-573-4
Ebook ISBN: 978-1-63450-974-9

Printed in China

To Joel and my beautiful children: Dallin, Caleb, Alaina, and Landon. You make life so much fun!

CONTENTS

INTRODUCTION

Why Craft?

There is just something special about creating with your own two hands. For children, making crafts is one of these special moments. Children are naturally creative creatures and crafting is a perfect outlet for their playful imaginations. Crafting also brings a sense of pride and makes a passing moment one they will remember forever. You will recognize this when a child holds up their completed craft to show you what they've made, and you see pure joy in their sweet little faces. It's an opportunity for them to shine.

Holiday Crafts

My first encounter with children's crafts began several years ago when I became a stay-at-home mom. I had a brand new baby and my oldest was about three years old. I loved being home with both my boys, but like many new stay-at-home moms, I soon discovered that I honestly didn't know what to do all day! As I was trying to find my new rhythm, I started coming up with simple crafts to do with my oldest son, Dallin. It was December and I had the idea to create one Christmas craft every day until Christmas. I'll always treasure the memories of this Christmas season and the special time Dallin and I had together crafting! Dallin and I had so much fun thinking up craft ideas that I wanted to share our ideas with others. I started a blog, LittleFamilyFun.com, where I posted all about our first adventure in advent crafting, and many more fun crafts and activities since.

Crafts are fun to make anytime of the year, but holiday crafts are just a little bit extra special. Maybe it's because holidays give us a reason and desire to do fun things (like make crafts!). Or maybe it's because holidays are filled with anticipation, and creating a fun holiday craft is a good way to channel all that excitement! Whatever the reason, crafts are a great way to celebrate special holidays and occasions all year-round.

How to Use This Book

This book includes crafts for ten holidays and special occasions that are exciting for children. There are five craft ideas for each holiday, complete with step-by-step instructions and photos. For easy preparation, each craft will include a blue box in the top right corner with a list of all supplies needed for that craft. Some crafts will also include a Tip Box at the bottom with some fun and useful ideas for creating and displaying that craft.

There are varying levels of crafts throughout this book. Most of them are simple enough to follow that older children could make many of these crafts all by themselves! Younger children, however, will most likely need someone there to help them along the way. Whether they need help or not, crafting is an easy and fun opportunity to be together as a family. In fact, that's my very favorite part about children's crafts! Crafting is a good reminder to slow down and sit down with my children. While my children are busy crafting away, we chat and laugh, and I'm filled with renewed gratitude that I get to be their mom.

Supplies

There are so many supplies available to make fun crafts, but crafting does not have to be complicated. For the purpose of simplicity, this book includes crafts that can be made with only eleven basic craft supplies that are inexpensive and that you can find easily in stores.

1. Construction Paper
2. Craft Foam
3. Paint
4. Yarn
5. Craft Sticks
6. Googly Eyes
7. Hole Punch
8. Scissors
9. Glue
10. Marker
11. Pencil

Here is a short description of these basic supplies:

Construction Paper

Construction paper is perhaps the number-one craft supply around. Since it comes in all colors, it can be used for any holiday, and can be folded, cut, and rolled in more ways than you can imagine! You will need a pad or package of construction paper with all these basic colors: red, orange, yellow, green, blue, purple, pink, white, black, and brown.

Craft Foam

Craft foam is so much fun to craft with. Since it is nice and thick, it's more durable than construction paper and also gives more dimension to crafts. Similar to the construction paper, you will need an assortment of colors: red, orange, yellow, green, blue, purple, pink, white, black, and brown.

Paint

The kind of paint that is best for kids' crafts is called by many names: finger paint, tempera paint, washable paint, etc. Basically, it is paint that is washable (meaning it won't stain clothes). It comes in various sizes, but if you're crafting with paint a lot, you might want to buy the 16 oz. bottles. For the crafts in this book, you'll need paint in these basic colors: red, orange, yellow, green, blue, purple, and white. Another option would be to just get the primary colors of red, yellow, and blue. You can then mix them together to get the other colors you need as follows: red + yellow = orange, yellow + blue = green, blue + red = purple.

Yarn

It's always good to have a couple bundles of yarn on hand. It can be used for making necklaces, lacing, and in many other fun ways you will discover throughout this book! There are some crafts in this book that specifically use white yarn, such as the Craft Stick Mummy (p. 87) and the Snowman Ornament (p. 115). For most of the others that call for yarn, you can use any color you have on hand, or mix and match your favorite colors.

Googly Eyes

These fun little eyes are also known as wiggle eyes or glue-on eyes. They come in a variety of sizes and definitely add a whole lot of cuteness to crafts. Some of the crafts tend to look a little better with the one-inch googly eyes, but any size will do for most of the crafts in this book.

Hole Punch

The hole punch referred to in this book is the handheld kind. It's a handy tool to have while crafting. It's not only good in creating holes for lacing yarn, it's also a great way to create small circles that are perfect for several other crafts in this book.

Scissors

This is perhaps the most useful tool of all and is needed for every single craft in this book. Get a good pair and use with care. Children should use age-appropriate scissors, and small children may need someone to do the scissor work for them.

Glue

You will use a lot of glue for the crafts in this book! I prefer bottled glue over glue sticks as it tends to stick longer and better.

Marker and Pencil

A black, washable marker is needed for a few crafts in this book as a way to give them a final, personal touch. A pencil is helpful in tracing or drawing the shapes you will need as you craft. It is also a very useful tool in rolling paper for several crafts in this book.

Now that you've got your supplies, it's time to craft!

*NOTE: With all craft supplies, please use caution in how children handle and use them. Small children will need more supervision and help with most of these supplies, especially scissors and small pieces, such as googly eyes.

CHAPTER 1

Valentine's Day

Paper Swirl Heart

Instructions:

1. Fold a piece of white construction paper in half and cut out half a heart shape.

Supplies:
- Construction Paper (white, red, and purple)
- Scissors
- Glue
- Pencil

2. Cut out strips of red and purple construction paper about one inch wide.

5. Put glue all over your white heart shape and begin placing the paper swirls all around the edge.

3. Take two strips at a time and roll them up around a pencil.

6. Keep placing the paper swirls on the heart until there's no room left. Let it dry and enjoy!

4. Roll up all the strips until you have enough paper swirls for your heart.

TIP: Hang this up as a Valentine's Day decoration, or give it as a special valentine to someone you love!

Heart Smile Valentines

Instructions:

Supplies:
- Construction Paper (white, yellow, and any color)
- Paint (purple)
- Scissors
- Glue
- Marker
- Pencil

1. Paint a piece of white construction paper with purple paint. Set it aside for a while and let it dry.

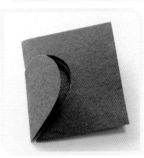

2. Fold a small piece of construction paper in half and cut out a heart, about two inches tall.

3. Trace this heart onto the painted purple paper and cut out as many hearts as you need.

4. Fold up a piece of yellow construction paper into eight equal parts. Then cut them out.

5. Glue a painted heart onto each piece of yellow paper. Draw eyes, a smile, arms, and legs onto each heart.

6. Then write the message, "You Make My Heart Smile." Hand them out as Valentines.

> **TIP:** If you need to make a lot of valentines, paint two pieces of paper with the purple paint so you can cut out enough hearts.

FOam Heart Card

Instructions:

1. Cut a piece of white construction paper in half, then fold each piece in half. Set one aside, and from the other, cut out half a heart shape, about five inches tall.

2. Cut out strips of craft foam from the three different colors, about one-third of an inch wide.

4. Turn over the heart and cut around the edges, trimming off the extra foam.

3. Place glue all over the heart. Then start placing the foam strips on the glue in a pattern. Let the glue dry.

5. Glue the foam-striped heart to the other piece of folded white paper. Then write a special valentine message on the inside!

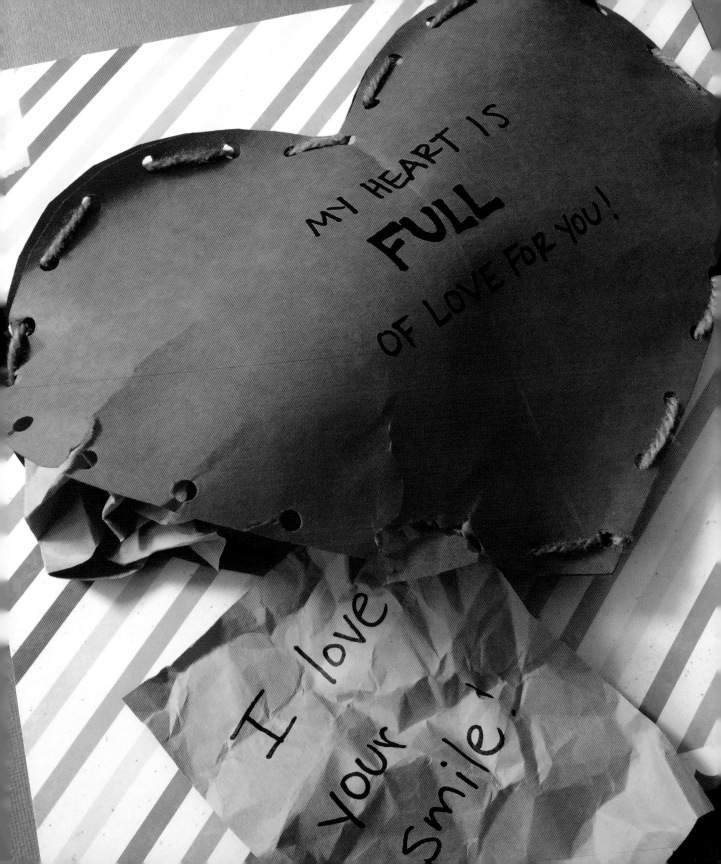

STUFFED HEART VALENTINE

Instructions:

1. Lay two pieces of red construction paper on top of each other and fold in half. Cut out half a heart shape.

2. Unfold, and on the top heart write the phrase, "My heart is FULL of love for you!"

3. Hold both hearts together and punch holes all along the edges of the hearts, about one inch apart.

4. Tie a knot with the yarn at the bottom of the heart and lace the rest of the yarn through all the holes. STOP when you have four holes left.

Supplies:
- Construction Paper (red and pink)
- Yarn (any color)
- Hole Punch
- Scissors
- Marker

5. Cut two pieces of pink construction paper into four rectangles each. Write special notes for your Valentine on each one, then scrunch them up.

6. Stuff the scrunched notes into the open end of the heart.

7. Finish lacing the heart and tie a knot. When you give it to your Valentine, tell them to rip it open to find a special surprise!

9

Hearts-on-a-string valentine

Instructions:

Supplies:
- Construction Paper
- Craft Foam (pink)
- Yarn
- Craft Sticks
- Hole Punch
- Scissors
- Glue
- Marker
- Pencil

1. Glue four craft sticks together at the ends, forming a square. Set aside and let dry completely.

2. Fold a small piece of construction paper in half and cut out a heart shape, about one to two inches tall.

3. Trace this shape onto pink craft foam and cut out three hearts.

4. Punch holes in each side of the hearts, then write the words, "I LOVE YOU!" with a marker.

5. Cut three pieces of yarn about ten inches long. Tie them each onto one of the sticks in a double knot. Then trim the ends off the extra yarn.

6. Thread the yarn through the holes of the hearts so the words are facing forward. Then tie the ends of the yarn to the opposite stick and trim the ends. All done!

CHAPTER 2

St. Patrick's Day

paper clover craft

Instructions:

1. Fold a piece of green construction paper in half and draw half of a four leaf clover. Then cut it out.

Supplies:
- Construction Paper (green)
- Scissors
- Glue

2. Unfold it and you've got a four-leaf clover!

4. Next, scrunch up all those scraps into little balls.

3. With another piece of green construction paper (and the scraps from the clover paper) cut up rectangles and squares. They don't have to match; just cut up some scraps.

5. Put glue all over the clover and place the scrunched up papers on top. Let it dry and enjoy!

TIP: In step one, pretend that you are drawing half of a butterfly. That will help you get a good clover shape! (This craft is also found on my blog, LittleFamilyFun.com.)

15

Painted Rainbow Collage

Supplies:
- Construction Paper (white)
- Paint (red, orange, yellow, green, blue, purple)
- Scissors
- Glue
- Marker

1. Get out six pieces of white construction paper and paint each one with the following colors: red, orange, yellow, green, blue, and purple. Let them dry completely.

2. Cut out squares from each painted paper, about one inch wide.

3. On another piece of white construction paper, draw a rainbow with six sections.

4. Starting with red on top, glue the painted squares onto each section of the rainbow.

5. When all the squares are glued on, you're all done!

TIP: If you don't have paint in all the colors of the rainbow, you can mix these colors together to get what you need!
Red + Yellow = Orange
Yellow + Blue = Green
Blue + Red = Purple

17

Craft Stick Leprechaun

Instructions:

1. Glue seven craft sticks to a piece of foam. This will hold them all in place.

Supplies:

- Craft Foam (green, black, orange, yellow, and brown)
- Craft Sticks
- Googly Eyes
- Scissors
- Glue
- Marker

2. Cut out a green rectangle as wide as the craft sticks and glue it to the top of the sticks. Then cut out several small orange rectangles and glue them below the green one.

4. Cut out and glue a black strip directly above the green strip. Then cut a yellow rectangle and cut out the middle. Glue this on top of the black strip.

3. Cut out and glue a long green strip directly below the green rectangle, and on top of the small orange rectangles.

5. Glue on two googly eyes and a brown circle for the nose. Then draw a smile with the marker and say hello to your lucky leprechaun!

POT-O-GOLD Craft

Instructions:

1. Fold a small piece of construction paper in half (any color), and cut out half a shape of a big pot.

Supplies:

- Construction Paper (red, orange, yellow, green, blue, purple)
- Craft Foam (white, black)
- Hole Punch
- Scissors
- Glue

2. Trace this shape onto black craft foam, cut it out, and glue it onto a piece of white craft foam.

3. Cut strips out of all the colors of construction paper, and glue these onto the white craft foam next to the big pot, making a rainbow.

4. Then trim off the paper strips hanging off the edge of the white foam.

5. Using a hole punch, make a pile of paper punches from the yellow construction paper. Put glue above the black pot and sprinkle the yellow punches onto the glue.

6. Put a few drops of glue down the side of the pot and on the ground, and sprinkle more yellow punches on the glue. Your treasure is complete!

GOOD LUCK CRaFT

Instructions:

1. Cut a piece of white craft foam six inches tall and four inches wide. Then cut five pieces of green craft foam one inch wide and four inches long.

2. Glue the green pieces on the white, about a quarter inch apart.

3. Fold a small piece of paper in half and cut out half a clover shape.

4. Trace the clover shape onto light green craft foam and cut it out. Punch a hole in the top and write, "GOOD LUCK."

5. Cut a piece of white yarn about ten inches long. Thread it through the clover.

6. Tie the yarn through the holes in the craft foam. Trim the ends off the knots. All done!

TIP: Drawing half of a four-leaf clover is kind of like drawing the letter B, with a little stem on the bottom.

23

CHAPTER 3

Easter

Peek-a-Boo Bunny

Instructions:

1. Glue seven craft sticks onto a piece of craft foam.

Supplies:

- Craft Foam (white, pink, and any other color)
- Craft Sticks
- Googly Eyes
- Scissors
- Glue
- Marker

2. Then glue a stick across the top, one across the bottom, and one diagonally from top to bottom. Now it looks like a fence!

4. Glue the big circle behind the sticks, and add the ears and nose. Then glue the small circles on top of the sticks on either side.

3. Out of white craft foam, cut out a big circle, two small circles, and two bunny ear shapes. Out of the pink foam, cut out two smaller bunny ear shapes, and a small circle for the nose.

5. Glue on the googly eyes and draw whiskers with a marker. Peek-a-boo!

PaPer EGG CraFT

Instructions:

1. Fold the purple piece of construction paper in half and cut out half an egg shape.

2. Unfold it and there's your egg!

3. Cut out long strips of yellow and pink construction paper, about one inch wide.

4. Fold each strip with the "accordion fold" where you fold a piece over, then fold it back the other way, all down the strip.

Supplies:

- Construction Paper (purple, pink, yellow)
- Scissors
- Glue

5. Put glue all over the egg and place the folded strips on top, alternating the pink and yellow colors. Lightly press down on the strips to help them stick to the glue.

6. Let the glue dry completely, then turn it over and cut around the egg shape, trimming off the extra strips hanging over the edge.

29

carrot Bracelet

Instructions:

Supplies:
- Construction Paper
- Craft Foam (orange, green)
- Scissors
- Glue
- Marker

1. Fold a piece of construction paper and cut out half a carrot shape, about eight inches long.

2. Unfold it and trace it onto a piece of craft foam. Cut it out.

3. Cut out a triangle from the green craft foam. Then fold it in half and cut two slits into it.

4. Glue the green triangle to the top of the foam carrot shape. Then trim the top of the triangle to have some jagged edges like leaves.

5. Draw a few lines of different lengths all down the carrot. This helps it look more carrot-like! Let the glue dry then you can wear it as a bracelet!

6. To wear it as a bracelet, simply wrap it around and tuck the pointy end of the carrot up the first slot and down the second slot on the green leaf.

ROLL-UP BUNNY

Instructions:

1. Cut a piece of white construction paper in half so you have two long pieces. Roll up one of the pieces around a pencil or marker.

2. Cut the other piece of white paper in half again, giving you another long piece, just not as wide. Wrap that around a pencil too. Then glue the smaller roll to the side of the bigger roll.

3. Cut out two white bunny-ear shapes, then two smaller pink bunny ear shapes. Glue the pink ones onto the white ones.

4. Fold under the bottom part of each ear and glue them to the smaller roll.

5. Cut out a small pink circle and glue it on as a nose. Then with a marker, draw eyes, mouth, and whiskers.

6. Let the glue dry. "Hoppy" Easter!

FLOWER STAMP EGG

Instructions:

Supplies:
- Construction Paper (any color)
- Paint (any color)
- Scissors
- Glue

1. Cut a piece of construction paper in half, then in half again. Place glue on one side of one of the papers.

2. Roll up the paper so that it forms a tube about one inch wide.

3. Make five cuts into one end of the tube, about one inch deep. Then fold out the pieces. This is your flower stamp!

4. Next, fold a piece of construction paper in half and cut out half an egg shape.

5. Put some paint onto a plate and dip the flower stamp into the paint. Then stamp flowers onto the egg.

6. Let the paint dry and you're all done!

TIP: This flower-stamp egg can be made with many different colors of paper and paint. The creative possibilities are endless! (This craft is also found on my blog, LittleFamilyFun.com.)

35

CHAPTER 4

Mother's Day

TULIP BOOK FOR MOM

Instructions:

1. Fold a small piece of construction paper in half and cut out a tulip shape, about four inches tall.

2. Trace the tulip shape two times onto three different colors of craft foam. Then cut two small leaf shapes out of green foam.

3. Punch two holes into the left-hand side of each tulip shape. On one shape write, "Mom, I love you because . . ."

4. On the rest of the tulips, write special things you love about your Mom.

Supplies:

- Construction Paper (any color)
- Craft Foam (yellow, light purple, dark purple, green)
- Yarn
- Craft Stick
- Hole Punch
- Scissors
- Glue
- Marker

5. Cut two pieces of yarn about four inches long. Thread them through each of the holes in the tulips and tie them in knots. Trim off the extra yarn.

6. Glue the tulip book to the top of a craft stick. Then glue the two leaf shapes on the sides of the craft stick. Give it to your mom along with a hug.

FOLDED FLOWERS CARD

Instructions:

1. Cut out three squares from the red construction paper, about two inches big. Fold them in half, then in half again.

Supplies:
- Construction Paper (white, red, blue)
- Scissors
- Glue
- Marker

2. Unfold them, then fold each corner of the squares to the opposite corners.

5. Glue the squares to the card, in the middle. Cut out small blue circles and glue them to the middle of each flower.

3. Fold a piece of white construction paper in half to form a card. On top write the words, "Happy Mother's Day!"

6. With the marker, draw stems and small leaves under each flower. Inside the card, write a special message for Mother's Day!

4. Place a drop of glue on the back of each square in the middle.

41

painted stripe card

Instructions:

1. Get out three pieces of white paper and paint them with each of the colors: red, purple, and yellow. Let the paint dry completely.

2. Cut the yellow and purple painted papers into strips, about one inch thick.

3. Fold a piece of white construction paper in half and start gluing the painted strips onto the front, alternating purple and yellow.

5. Fold the piece of red painted paper in half and cut out half a heart shape, about three inches tall.

6. Glue the red heart on top of the stripes. Then write a special message for Mother's Day inside the card!

4. Let the glue dry then trim the edges around the card.

MOM
YOU MAKE MY
HEART
ALL WARM AND
FUZZY!

warm and Fuzzy Heart

Instructions:

1. Fold a small piece of construction paper in half and cut out a heart shape, about three inches tall.

Supplies:
- Construction Paper (any color)
- Craft Foam (white)
- Yarn (any color)
- Scissors
- Glue
- Marker

2. Trace the heart onto the bottom of a piece of white craft foam. Then above it write the words, "Mom, You make my heart all warm and FUZZY!"

3. Put glue all over inside the heart shape. Then start snipping very small pieces off the end of a long piece of yarn.

4. Fill the entire inside of the heart with trimmings from the yarn. This will make the heart look nice and fuzzy.

5. Let the glue dry; then you're all done!

TIP: You could also make this into a card! Instead of using craft foam, fold a piece of paper in half and decorate it the same way!

45

FLOWER SWIRL CRAFT

Instructions:

Supplies:
- Construction Paper (white, yellow, green, purple)
- Scissors
- Glue
- Pencil

1. Cut out five strips of white construction paper, und one strip of yellow construction paper, about half an inch wide. Roll them all up around a pencil.

2. Unroll them from each other and set them aside.

3. Cut a piece of purple construction paper in half. Then put glue on the top half, in the shape of a flower with five petals.

4. Place all five of the white paper swirls on the glue, then the yellow one in the middle.

5. From the green paper cut out two long paper strips, and one short one. Roll the two long strips around a pencil.

6. Glue the short green strip under the flower for the stem, and the two rolled strips on the sides as leaves. Give it to your mom for Mother's Day!

CHAPTER 5

Father's Day

FATHER'S DAY TIE CARD

Instructions:

1. Cut a piece of construction paper in half, then fold that part in half. Draw and cut out half of a tie shape, as shown.

Supplies:
- Construction Paper (white, and any other colors)
- Craft Foam (any color)
- Hole Punch
- Scissors
- Glue

2. Unfold the tie shape and trace it onto a piece of craft foam. Then cut it out.

3. Punch holes out of a piece of construction paper and set them in a pile.

4. Put glue all over the tie and sprinkle the paper circles on top.

5. Cut a piece of white construction paper in half the long way, fold it over, and make a cut on each side at the top, about one inch long.

6. Glue the tie onto the paper and fold the top pieces together to look like the collar of a shirt. You can open the card from the bottom and write a special message inside!

Painted Dad Card

Instructions:

1. Write the word "DAD" onto the top half of a white piece of construction paper.

Supplies:

- Construction Paper (white, yellow, and any color)
- Craft Foam (any color)
- Paint (blue)
- Scissors
- Glue
- Pencil

2. Cut a square out of any color of construction paper and scrunch it up into a ball.

3. Dip the scrunched-up paper into some blue paint and stamp it onto the letters on the white paper.

4. Let the paint dry completely. Then cut out the painted letters.

5. Cut out nine small squares of craft foam and glue three to the back of each of the letters. This will make them pop out a little bit.

6. Fold a piece of yellow construction paper in half and glue the letters on top. Inside the card, write a special message for Father's Day!

MONSTER TRUCK CRAFT

Instructions:

Supplies:
- Craft Foam (red, white, black, yellow)
- Scissors
- Glue
- Marker

1. Cut a basic truck shape out of red craft foam as shown in the picture to the left.

2. Round out the corners on the top and front end of the truck.

5. Glue on the black triangle, and a small yellow circle for a headlight.

3. Cut out two big black circles and two smaller white circles. Glue them together and write the words as shown.

6. Glue the wheels onto the truck. Then write "DAD" on the truck. Give this as a fun Father's Day card!

4. Cut out a small black triangle and then trim out the inside. This will go in the back of the truck.

> **TIP:** For the wheels, find two cups of different sizes. Press the larger cup into the black foam, and the smaller cup into the white foam. Then you can easily cut out the circles following the imprints you made with the cups!

STICK SIGN FOR DAD

Instructions:

1. Lay out five craft sticks and line them up next to each other. Then glue one craft stick down the middle of all of them. Let the glue dry, then turn it over. This is your stick sign.

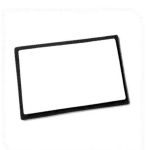

2. Cut out two rectangles from craft foam: a blue one to fit onto the stick sign and a white one just smaller than the blue one.

3. With a black marker, write a message for dad on the white rectangle, then glue it to the blue one.

4. Cut two small hearts out of the red craft foam and glue them around your message.

5. Glue the rectangles onto the craft sticks. Let it all dry and give it to your dad for Father's Day!

TIP: You could even stick this cute little sign into the top of a cake for Father's Day!

Race car card

Instructions:

1. Cut out a small car shape from three colors of craft foam.

2. Punch holes on both ends of each car. Then write the words "Happy Father's Day" on the cars.

5. Cut three long pieces of yarn. Thread them through the holes on the left, then through the holes on the cars.

3. Cut out six small circles from the black craft foam. Glue them onto the back of each car.

6. Thread the other ends of the yarn through the holes on the right. Then tie them together in the back. All done!

4. On a rectangle of white craft foam, write the words, "We're RACING to say...". Then punch three holes on each side.

59

CHAPTER 6

Fourth of July

FOLDED RECTANGLE FLAG

Instructions:

1. Cut out rectangles from the construction paper about two inches by four inches. You will need four blue, ten red, and ten white.

2. Wrap each rectangle around a craft stick one or two at a time.

3. Take them off the craft stick and glue the edges together to form a square shape.

4. Do this with all of the papers and set them aside to dry.

Supplies:

- Construction Paper (red, white, and blue)
- Craft Stick
- Hole Punch
- Scissors
- Glue

5. Cut a white piece of construction paper in half and put glue on the top half. Start with the blue papers and place them on the glue in the pattern of an American flag.

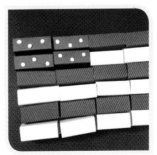

6. Punch out a few holes of white paper and glue them onto the blue rectangles to look like "stars." Your flag is finished!

Patriotic Pal

Instructions:

Supplies:
- Craft Foam (red, white, and blue)
- Googly Eyes
- Scissors
- Glue
- Marker

1. Cut out the following shapes from craft foam:
- One blue square
- Three long blue strips
- Three long white strips
- Three long red strips
- Four small blue rectangles
- Two white circles
- Two red circles

4. Glue on the googly eyes and with a black marker draw a smile. All done! Say hello to your new pal!

2. Place glue on the blue square and put on the long strips in the pattern of red, white, then blue. Let the glue dry.

3. Trim off the extra foam around the blue square. Then glue on the rectangles as arms and legs, and the circles as hands and feet.

> **TIP:** The fun thing about this patriotic pal is you can make it as big or as small as you like! If you make it big, you could hang it on the wall for a fun decoration. If you make it small, you could glue on a craft stick to turn it into a puppet. You could also glue a magnet on the back and put it on the fridge!

Triangle Wreath

Instructions:

Supplies:
- Construction Paper (red, white, blue)
- Scissors
- Glue
- Yarn (optional)

1. Cut out eight triangles from each of the colors of paper: red, white, and blue. Set aside.

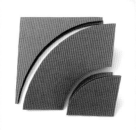

2. Cut a big square out of red construction paper. Fold it in half, then in half again. Cut a round line from corner to corner around the center. Then another round line about an inch below that. Unfold it and you've got your circle for the wreath.

3. Start gluing the triangles onto the circle in the pattern of red, white, and blue.

4. After you've gone around the circle once, layer another set of triangles in the same pattern on top.

5. Let it dry. If you want to hang it up as a decoration, you can glue a piece of yarn to the back.

Firework Art

Instructions:

1. Cut a long piece of yarn and wrap it around three of your fingers until you get to the end.

2. Take it off your fingers and tie another piece of yarn down the middle. Then cut the loops on both sides.

3. Fluff the yarn pieces out. Then do the same thing two more times, so you have three yarn balls. These will be what you paint with to make it look like fireworks!

4. Take one of the yarn balls and dip it into red paint. Then stamp it onto the black piece of construction paper several times. Then do the same with the other yarn balls in the white and blue paint.

5. Let it dry and enjoy your painted firework scene!

TIP: You could also make this into a card, and write a message inside wishing someone a happy Fourth of July

yarn star

Instructions:

1. Cut a star shape out of construction paper: half a point at the top, a point to the side, and a point diagonally down.

2. Trace the star onto red craft foam. Cut it out. Then punch holes into each point of the star: one at the top, and one on each side.

3. Cut about eight pieces each of blue and white yarn. They should be about twelve inches long.

4. Thread a piece of blue yarn through a top hole, and two pieces of white yarn through the side holes. Wrap the yarn around the bottom of the star.

5. Tie the ends together in a knot then trim the ends. Then do the same thing on the next point, alternating the white and blue threads.

6. Turn it over and see the cool design you've created on your star!

TIP: If you want to hang up this cute star, tie another piece of yarn through the top hole and tie it into a loop.

71

CHAPTER 7

Back to School

APPLE CHAIN

Instructions:

1. Fold a small piece of construction paper in half and cut out a "C" shape. Then from that cut out the middle.

2. Trace this "C" shape onto more pieces of green and red construction paper. Cut them out and unfold them. These are your apples!

3. Cut through the top of each apple shape. Then start linking the apples together.

4. From the brown paper cut out small rectangles for the stems and leaf shapes out of the green paper.

5. When the apples are all linked together in a chain, glue stems on the top to close the opening of each apple. Then add the leaf next to the stem. Hang it up as a fun back-to-school decoration!

TIP: This can also be a fun way to count down the days until school starts. You could start it a week or two before the first day of school, and cut an apple off the chain each day!

75

CURLED APPLE NECKLACE

Instructions:

1. Cut a long strip of red construction paper, about two inches wide. Wrap it around a pencil.

Supplies:

- Construction Paper (red, brown, green)
- Yarn
- Scissors
- Glue
- Pencil

2. Unroll it from the pencil and set it aside.

3. Cut out a stem shape from the brown paper, and a leaf shape from the green paper. Fold the ends of them so they will stand up when you glue them onto the apple.

4. Glue the stem and leaf onto the paper roll.

5. Cut a long piece of yarn and thread it through the paper roll. Tie the ends and try on your new apple necklace!

> **TIP:** Another version of this necklace could be to roll up even more red papers so you have the whole necklace covered in apple-rolls.

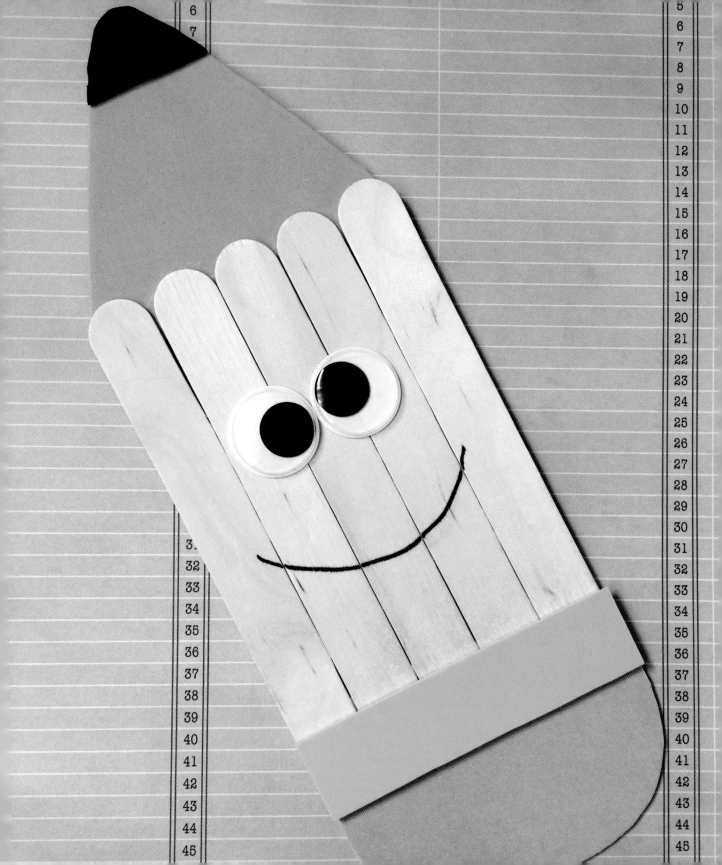

PENCIL PAL

Instructions:

1. Lay out five craft sticks in a row. Cut a square of craft foam and glue it onto all the sticks. This will keep them all together.

Supplies:

- Craft Foam (tan, black, pink, green)
- Craft Sticks
- Googly Eyes
- Scissors
- Glue
- Marker

2. Cut out the following craft foam pieces the same width as the sticks:
- A tan triangle with a rounded tip
- A green rectangle
- A pink square with two rounded corners
- A small black triangle with a rounded tip.

3. Glue the tan triangle behind the top of the sticks. Then glue the small black triangle to the tip.

4. Glue the pink piece behind the sticks on the bottom, then the green rectangle on top of the sticks.

5. Glue on two googly eyes, and draw a smile with a marker. All done! Say hello to your Pencil Pal!

APPLE PUPPETS

Instructions:

1. Fold a piece of construction paper in half and cut out a "C" shape. Unfold it and you have an apple!

2. Trace this apple shape onto red and green craft foam, then cut them out.

3. Cut out three brown rectangles for the stems, and three green leaves.

4. Glue the stems and leaves to the backs of the apples. Then glue a craft stick onto the back of each apple. Let them dry.

5. Draw eyes and a smile on the front of each apple, then put on a puppet show!

TIP: Not only are these apple puppets a fun craft to make, they are also fun to PLAY with! You can make as many as you want and put on a puppet show! Or you can make up songs to sing with them. You can also use them to practice counting. So many fun possibilities! (This craft is also found on my blog, LittleFamilyFun.com.)

SCHOOL BUS Name

Instructions:

1. Paint a piece of construction paper with yellow paint. Let it dry.

Supplies:

- Construction Paper (white, black)
- Paint (yellow)
- Scissors
- Glue
- Marker

2. Cut out a simple shape of a bus, as shown in the picture.

4. Glue on the wheels and stripes. Then glue on the rectangles as windows.

3. From the black construction paper, cut out two big circles, and two long skinny stripes. From the white construction paper cut out several rectangles— however many you need for each letter of your name.

5. With a black marker, write the letters of your name on the windows of the bus. *Vroom vroom!* You're all done!

> **TIP:** Depending on how long your name is, your windows may need to be smaller in order to fit them all on the bus.

CHAPTER 8

Halloween

CRAFT STICK MUMMY

Instructions:

1. Begin wrapping the yarn around a craft stick, securing the loose end under the yarn as you wrap.

Supplies:
- Yarn (white)
- Craft Sticks
- Googly Eyes
- Scissors
- Glue

2. Wrap the entire stick. Then cut the yarn and tuck the loose end under another piece of yarn.

4. Let it dry and enjoy! All done!

3. Glue two googly eyes on top of the yarn.

TIP: These little mummies are cute all by themselves. Or for added fun, you could try one of the following:
- Make a card! Glue them onto a piece of folded construction paper and write: "Happy Halloween!"
- Decorate! Use them for Halloween decorations by sticking them into a garden pot with soil.
- Party favors! Hand them out as party favors at your next Halloween party.

Paper Roll Pumpkin

• •

Instructions:

Supplies:
- Construction Paper (orange, green, white)
- Scissors
- Glue

1. Squeeze glue onto half a piece of orange construction paper.

2. From the opposite end, start rolling the paper toward the glue, making a circle tube about one inch wide.

3. After the glue dries, cut the entire paper tube about every half inch creating lots of little paper circles.

4. Next, fold a piece of white construction paper in half and cut out a simple pumpkin shape, as shown.

5. Unfold it, put glue all over it, and begin placing the paper circles all over the glue.

6. Roll up a piece of green construction paper and glue it on for the stem. Happy Halloween!

TIP: You can make this pumpkin as big or small as you like! Just roll up more orange paper if you need more circles! (This craft is also found on my blog, LittleFamilyFun.com.)

MIX-UP MONSTER

Instructions:

1. Cut out the following shapes from any colors of craft foam:
- One large circle
- One medium circle
- Two small circles
- Four small circles
- One large square
- One medium square
- Two small squares
- Four small squares.

Supplies:

- Craft Foam (any colors)
- Googly Eyes
- Scissors
- Glue
- Marker

2. On the medium-sized square and circle, glue on different amounts of googly eyes to make them look like monsters. Then draw a smile.

3. You now have what you need to create many different combinations of monsters!

4. Mix and match the large shapes as the bodies, and the small shapes for the arms and legs.

5. When you find a combination that you like, you can glue them onto a piece of paper. Or, instead of gluing them down, you can place them in a small bag and pull them out when you want to build your own unique monster. Have fun!

FINGERPRINT SKELETON

Instructions:

1. Draw a stick figure onto a piece of black paper.

Supplies:
- Construction Paper (black)
- Paint (white)
- Scissors
- Marker

2. Dip your finger into white paint and put fingerprints all along the lines of the stick figure.

4. Cut the figure out by cutting around all the fingerprints. All done!

3. Then put two fingerprints on the face for eyes, and a few small fingerprints underneath for a smile. Let the paint dry.

TIP: This skeleton craft is so simple and fun to make! You could also fold a piece of black paper in half and make a Halloween card with this fingerprint skeleton on the front!

GHOST FINGER PUPPET

Instructions:

1. Cut out two "U" shapes from white craft foam. These need to be big enough to fit on your finger.

Supplies:
- Craft Foam (white)
- Yarn (any color)
- Hole Punch
- Scissors
- Marker

2. Turn them around, and trim the bottoms to look like the bottom of a ghost.

3. Hold the two pieces together and punch holes all along the outside edges.

4. Cut a long piece of yarn. Thread it through the first hole and tie a knot. Then lace it through all the holes. On the last hole, tie a knot and trim off the extra yarn.

5. Draw two eyes and a smile on the front. You can now put your finger inside and enjoy your new puppet!

> TIP: You can make just one ghost puppet, or several. These are fun to play with. You can sing songs with them, or practice counting!

CHAPTER 9

Thanksgiving

POP-OUT TURKEY

Instructions:

1. Cut out eight brown circles and fold them each in half.

2. Put glue on the side of one of the circles and glue it to the side of another circle.

3. Glue all the circles together this way. This creates a fun pop-out for the turkey's body!

4. Cut out a circle in each of the colors: green, purple, and orange. Then cut them each in half.

Supplies:
- Construction Paper (brown, green, purple, orange, red)
- Scissors
- Glue
- Marker

5. Lay one of each half circle facing down on the left, and the others facing down on the right. Put glue on the bottom edges.

6. Place the pop-out circles on the glue. Cut out a small brown circle for the head. Draw eyes with a marker, and glue on a beak and small red piece under the beak.

7. Glue the head on. Lastly, cut out and glue on two orange legs. *Gobble, gobble.* You're all done!

PILGRIM PUPPET

Instructions:

1. Glue two craft sticks together—the middle of one onto the top half of the other one. Leave a little bit of stick above.

Supplies:

- Craft Foam (black, white, tan, yellow, brown)
- Craft Sticks
- Googly Eyes
- Scissors
- Glue
- Marker

2. Using black craft foam, cut out a shirt shape to fit onto the sticks. Then add a white collar and three white circles for buttons.

5. Glue the hat pieces on. Below the hat, glue two small brown triangles for hair, eyes, and a circle nose.

3. Cut out a tan circle and glue it on above the shirt. This is the pilgrim's head.

6. Draw a smile with a black marker and you're all done!

4. Cut out the pieces of a pilgrim hat to fit the head shape you glued on, as shown in the picture.

TIP: You can use this puppet to tell about the first Thanksgiving, sing songs with, or anything else fun!

painted indian corn

Instructions:

1. Cut out a few rectangles from the green paper.

Supplies:
- Construction Paper (green, white)
- Paint (red, orange, yellow)
- Scissors
- Glue
- Pencil

2. One at a time, roll them around a pencil and glue them so they form small rolls.

5. Cover the corn shape with all the different colors and let it dry (overnight is good).

3. Fold a piece of white paper in half. Cut out half of a tall corn shape.

6. Cut out two big leaf shapes from the green paper.

4. Unfold the corn shape. Then dip each of the green paper rolls into the different colors of paint. Stamp them all over the corn shape.

7. Glue the leaves on the bottom of the corn. Looks good enough to eat (but don't)!

103

Mayflower Craft

Instructions:

1. Cut a long piece of dark blue paper into small peaks to look like waves on the sea. Then glue it onto a piece of light blue paper.

Supplies:
- Construction Paper (light blue, dark blue, brown, white)
- Scissors
- Glue
- Marker

2. Cut a boat shape out of a piece of brown paper. Glue it on top of the blue papers.

5. Roll each of the brown rectangles and glue the edges down. Let them dry for a few minutes.

3. Using the white paper, cut out two shapes to look like sails on the boat. Glue them above the boat, and draw lines with a marker.

6. Glue these paper rolls onto the boat. They will resemble the logs used to make the *Mayflower*!

4. Cut out a pile of brown rectangles, about ten or so.

TIP: Depending on how big your boat is, you many need more "logs." Just add as many as you need to cover the boat so it can sail the ocean blue!

PILGrim HaT

1. Using black craft foam, cut out a long strip with the edges cut at a slant. Then cut out a triangle with the top cut off. Glue this onto the strip. This will make your pilgrim hat!

2. Cut out a thin white strip and glue it onto the bottom of the triangle shape. Then cut a yellow rectangle and cut out the middle to make the buckle. Glue this onto the white strip.

3. Let the glue dry for a few minutes.

Supplies:

- Construction Paper (black)
- Craft Foam (black, white, yellow)
- Scissors
- Glue

5. Cut two long strips of black construction paper.

6. Glue the ends of the two strips together. Glue the pilgrim hat on top of this and let it dry. Measure the strips around your head and glue the strips together in the back to form a circle. Let it all dry. Then you can put on your pilgrim hat!

CHAPTER 10

Christmas

present wreath

Instructions:

Supplies:
- Craft Foam (red and green)
- Scissors
- Glue

1. Cut out three red squares, three green squares, six green strips, and six red strips.

2. Cut out three small rectangles of red, and three of green. Fold them in half and cut triangle shapes, but don't cut all the way together at the tip.

3. When you unfold them, they will be the bows.

4. Glue the red strips and bows onto the green squares, and the green strips and bows onto the red squares. Let them dry completely.

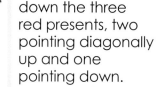

5. To create your wreath, lay down the three red presents, two pointing diagonally up and one pointing down.

6. Put glue on the bottom corners of each present then place the green presents on the corners of the red presents. Let it dry completely. Then glue on a piece of yarn to hang it up.

TIP: You can make this wreath any size you wish! If your presents are big, you can hang this on your door or in a window. If your presents are small, you could turn this into an ornament and hang it on your tree!

111

Triangle Tree

Instructions:

1. Cut a piece of green paper into six equal rectangles.

Supplies:

- Construction Paper (green, pink)
- Craft Foam (yellow)
- Craft Stick
- Scissors
- Glue

2. Leave one paper as it is. Then cut about one inch off the next, two inches off the next, and so on until you get to the last paper. It will be about one inch wide.

3. One at a time, wrap each paper around a craft stick. Unfold it and glue the edges together to form a triangle.

4. Glue the longest triangle piece about one inch from the bottom of the craft stick, then the next longest, and so on up to the top.

5. Cut a star shape out of yellow craft foam and glue it to the very top of the craft stick.

6. Cut out several small triangles from pink paper. Place a dot of glue on them and glue them to the edges of the triangles of the tree. All done!

> **TIP:** You could also turn this into a Christmas ornament by looping a piece of yarn through the top triangle!

113

yarn snowman ornament

Instructions:

Supplies:
- Construction Paper (black)
- Craft Foam (white, orange)
- Yarn (white)
- Hole Punch
- Scissors
- Glue

1. Cut out a circle from the white craft foam. Begin wrapping yarn around it, going in all different directions.

2. When you've got enough yarn wrapped around to cover most of the craft foam, cut the yarn and tie it in the back.

3. Cut a smaller circle of white craft foam and do the same thing. Then tie the two circles together with a small piece of yarn wrapped through the yarn of both circles, pulled tight, and tied in a knot.

4. Cut out a small triangle from the orange craft foam and glue it on for the nose. Punch out two small circles from the black paper using a hole punch. Glue them on for eyes.

5. Punch out three more circles and glue them onto the large circle for buttons. Tie a piece of yarn through the top circle and tie the ends together. Now you can hang it on your Christmas tree!

HanDPrint canDy cane

Instructions:

1. Draw a very small cane shape on the middle of a white piece of paper.

2. Draw a larger cane shape a couple inches above that. Then connect them together with rounded lines on the top and bottom. This is a simple way to draw a big candy cane.

3. Cut out your candy cane shape.

Supplies:

- Construction Paper (white)
- Paint (red)
- Scissors
- Pencil

4. Dip your hand in red paint and stamp it from one end of the candy cane to the other. Let it dry.

5. When the paint is all dry, the red handprints will make it look like the stripes on a candy cane!

TIP: You could also add another color of paint if you want it more colorful! Create a pattern of red and green handprints all over the candy cane. Or you could try red and pink handprints. (This craft is also found on my blog, LittleFamilyFun.com.)

ELF HaT

Instructions:

Supplies:
- Craft Foam (red, green)
- Yarn (white)
- Hole Punch
- Scissors
- Glue

1. Cut out a big triangle from red craft foam. Starting one inch from the bottom, punch holes about one inch apart along the tall edges of the triangle.

2. Cut a long piece of yarn. Lace the yarn through the top hole on the hat and tie a knot.

3. Lace the other end of the yarn through the next hole, then across the hat to the next hole on the other side. Continue all the way to the last hole. Tie a knot and trim the end off. Set it aside.

4. Wrap a long piece of yarn around a few of your fingers. Take it off your fingers and tie a piece of yarn in the middle.

5. Cut the loops and fluff it out. Then tie one of these pieces of yarn through the top hole and tie a knot.

6. Finally, cut a strip of green craft foam about one inch wide. Trim the ends upward and glue it to the bottom of the triangle. Merry Christmas!

119

ACKNOWLEDGEMENTS

There is so much gratitude in my heart for all those who have helped and supported me as I worked on this book.

My husband Joel has been my biggest supporter, fan, and best friend throughout this process and in every aspect of my life. I love you Joel with all my heart!

My children Dallin, Caleb, Alaina, and Landon is how it all began. We're all crafting buddies and it is because of them that my blog and this book were ever created. Their excitement, energy, and imagination brings so much joy to my life. I love you sweetie pies!

My parents Vic and Betty Erickson have always been my heroes. They've been my support and strength all throughout my life. Their examples of faith, determination and love have shaped me. I love you Mom and Dad!

My siblings, Laura, Lance, Lane, Lynn, Lisa, and Luke are such blessings in my life. I look up to each of you and have always felt love and support from you and your families. I love you all!

My extended family David & Becky Reece and all my in-law families have been so thoughtful and caring. I love you!

My friends near and far that have cheered for me, helped me, and inspired me along this path. Thank you.

The publishing team at Skyhorse Publishing, Julia Abramoff and Alexandra Hess, and everyone else on the crew. Thank you for this amazing opportunity and all your work!

And finally, my heart is full of humble gratitude to my loving Father in Heaven and Savior who have been near me and provided just what I need for every single day.

Index